JASPER'S
Secret

ISBN: 978-1-950791-05-7

Cover and text layout design: Kristi Yoder

Artist: Eva Zimmerman

Printed in China

Published by:

TGS International
P.O. Box 355
Berlin, Ohio 44610 USA
Phone: 330.893.4828
Fax: 330.893.2305
www.tgsinternational.com

JASPER'S
Secret

Written and illustrated by Eva Zimmerman

Introduction

Jasper's Secret is a true story about a growing pup that found a new friend. Charlotte is a Miniature Mediterranean baby donkey that liked to frisk and play. When Charlotte's mother grew tired of her antics, she gave her baby a firm nip with her teeth. So Charlotte was more than happy to have Jasper to frisk and play with.

Rows of trees on both sides of the green meadow hid Jasper and Charlotte safely from sight, and their friendship stayed a secret. Almost.

I hope you will enjoy hearing about Jasper and Charlotte.

—Eva Zimmerman

Jasper was a mostly black puppy. Only his chest, his four feet, and the very tip of his tail were white. Jasper belonged to a boy who liked to run and play almost as much as Jasper did. Oh, the fun those two had!

They hunted groundhogs and rabbits. They went swimming and fishing in the big creek. They found secret hiding places in the green meadow.

But the boy could not always play with Jasper. Sometimes there was work to do. Sometimes there were places to go. Sometimes there were books to read. Then the day came that the boy went to school. And Jasper was lonely.

So Jasper went to the green meadow to chase mice. He crept into the tall grass, and there he waited and waited. Only his black tail with a white tip moved. Back and forth, back and forth it went.

Then Jasper saw a mouse. Jump! Sometimes he missed. Then the mouse ran down, down into a tunnel deep under the roots of the tall grass. Sometimes he did not miss. Then he played and played with the mouse. Jasper chased mice hour after happy hour. But Jasper was still lonely.

So Jasper went to the big creek.
Into the cool water of the big
creek he splashed.

The sun was shining and shadows danced on the water. Under the water, little fish swam in and out of the shadows. In and out they swam, in and out.

Jasper could see the little fish swimming in the water. How he wanted to catch them! Jump! Jasper's head splashed under the water. Jump! Again and again. But Jasper never caught a fish. Not even one.

Jasper chased fish in the cool waters of the big creek, hour after happy hour. But Jasper was still lonely.

And then, Jasper found something.

Something special.

Across the big creek were more green meadows. Here Blue Hen came with her babies. And here is where Jasper found his special secret—a baby he had never seen before.

This baby was black, even more black than Jasper was. She had long legs—even longer than Jasper's legs. She had long ears—even longer than Jasper's ears. And this baby wanted to play—just as much as Jasper did!

Charlotte was a baby donkey. She lived in the barn where Blue Hen and her babies lived. Every day she went out into the green meadow with her mama. Every day she ran and jumped and played.

But Charlotte did not have anyone to play with. Her mama did not want to play all day long. Mama donkeys eat grass all day long.

Blue Hen and her babies did not want to play the whole day. Hens and chicks chase bugs all day long.

Then Charlotte saw a puppy—a black puppy with a white tip on his tail. Back and forth went that puppy's tail. Back and forth went that tail with a white tip. This puppy wanted to play! Oh, yes, he did! All day long.

The two babies walked closer together.
At last they were close enough to touch noses.
"Sniff!" went one pointy black nose.
"Sniff!" went one soft black nose.
"Sniff, sniff," went two black noses.

Then Mama Donkey saw Jasper. She did not like that he was so close to her baby. She thought he might hurt her baby. She ran at Jasper and stamped her two front feet. She chased him all the way to the big creek. Then she went back to eating grass in the green meadow.

But Jasper was still lonely. Slowly, slowly, he came
back. Charlotte wanted to play. Slowly, slowly,
she came toward Jasper. Mama Donkey was
busy eating. She did not see Jasper with her baby.
Charlotte kicked up her heels. Jasper liked that! He
ran toward Charlotte. Away they went across the
green meadows as fast as the wind! Past Blue Hen
and her babies, past the fish in the creek, past the
mice in the tall grass, past Mama Donkey they ran.

Mama Donkey saw them running. She saw that Jasper was not hurting her baby. She went right on eating grass and let them play. Now Jasper was not lonely! He had a special secret friend to play with! Oh, what a happy day!

Day after happy day Jasper crossed the big
creek into the meadow where Charlotte was.
Day after happy day the two friends played
together in the warm sunshine.

Jasper made sure he went home before the
boy came home from school. No one saw
Jasper going to play with his friend. No one but
Mama Donkey knew about the secret. It was
Jasper's secret. It was a happy secret. And
Jasper never told anyone. Not even the boy.

Jasper had been lonely. He had chased mice, but he was still lonely. He had chased fish, but he was still lonely. Then Jasper found a friend, a special friend.

Sometimes things are lonely.
Even when the sun shines.
Even when people are kind.
Then Someone is a special
friend.

Jesus is everyone's special friend. Jesus calls His children friends when they do what He wants them to do. Jesus shows His friends everything they need to know about God.

"Ye are my friends, if ye do whatsoever
I command you. . . . I have called you
friends; for all things that I have heard of
my Father I have made known unto you."
John 15:14–15

THE END

About the Author

Eva Zimmerman lives in Lancaster County, Pennsylvania, where she taught special education for 25 years. She enjoyed reading picture books to her students.

She has enjoyed the animals that have lived at her home over the years. Their antics and unique personalities have provided her with many stories to tell.

Her hobbies include bird watching, nature walks, drawing, painting, and carving. She also enjoys entertaining children.

Eva desires to use her talents to the honor and glory of God. She is the author of *Blue Hen*, also published by CAM. You can contact Eva by writing to her in care of Christian Aid Ministries, P. O. Box 360, Berlin, OH 44610.

About Christian Aid Ministries

Christian Aid Ministries was founded in 1981 as a nonprofit, tax-exempt 501(c)(3) organization. Its primary purpose is to provide a trustworthy and efficient channel for Amish, Mennonite, and other conservative Anabaptist groups and individuals to minister to physical and spiritual needs around the world. This is in response to the command to "... do good unto all men, especially unto them who are of the household of faith" (Galatians 6:10).

Each year, CAM supporters provide 15–20 million pounds of food, clothing, medicines, seeds, Bibles, Bible story books, and other Christian literature for needy people. Most of the aid goes to orphans and Christian families. Supporters' funds also help to clean up and rebuild for natural disaster victims, put up Gospel billboards in the U.S., support several church-planting efforts, operate two medical clinics, and provide resources for needy families to make their own living. CAM's main purposes for providing aid are to help and encourage God's people and bring the Gospel to a lost and dying world.

CAM has staff, warehouses, and distribution networks in Romania, Moldova, Ukraine, Haiti, Nicaragua, Liberia, Israel, and Kenya. Aside from management, supervisory personnel, and bookkeeping operations, volunteers do most of the work at CAM locations. Each year, volunteers at our warehouses, field bases, Disaster Response Services projects, and other locations donate over 200,000 hours of work.

CAM's ultimate purpose is to glorify God and help enlarge His kingdom. "... whatsoever ye do, do all to the glory of God" (1 Corinthians 10:31).